WHAT AND WHY WE BELIEVE

by

HARRY DEAN

BELIEF IN GOD
A study in the Christian idea of the Godhead

and

THE FAITH WE DECLARE
Brief studies in Salvation Army doctrine

Salvation Books
The Salvation Army International Headquarters
London, United Kingdom

Belief in God
First published 1961

The Faith We Declare
First published 1955
Second impression 1960
Third impression 1962

Both reprinted with some revision 2009

Copyright © 2009
The General of The Salvation Army

ISBN 978-0-85412-799-3

Unless otherwise stated, all scriptural quotes are taken from
THE HOLY BIBLE, NEW INTERNATIONAL VERSION

Copyright © 1973, 1978, 1984 by International Bible Society.
Used by permission of Zondervan.
All rights reserved.

Published by Salvation Books
The Salvation Army International Headquarters
101 Queen Victoria Street, London EC4V 4EH
United Kingdom

Printed by UK Territory Print & Design Unit

Contents

SERIES INTRODUCTION		v
FOREWORD		vii

Belief in God

1.	THE BEING OF GOD	1
2.	GOD MADE MANIFEST	11
3.	GOD IN MAN	19

The Faith We Declare

	INTRODUCTION	29
1.	THE BIBLE	31
2.	BELIEF IN GOD	35
3.	THE TRINITY	39
4.	JESUS, HUMAN AND DIVINE	41
5.	THE SIN OF MAN	45
6.	THE ATONEMENT	49
7.	THE CONDITIONS OF SALVATION	53
8.	JUSTIFICATION BY FAITH	57
9.	THE WAY OF OBEDIENCE	61
10.	THE SANCTIFIED LIFE	65
11.	LAST THINGS	69

SERIES INTRODUCTION

'CLASSIC SALVATIONIST TEXTS'

This series is intended to help a new generation of readers become familiar with works published across the years by The Salvation Army and which over time have come to be regarded as 'classics' in Salvationist circles and even beyond. It is hoped also that these republications might lead to a rediscovery of them and the truths they convey by those who once read them. They live on not only for their content, but also for the passionate spirit that breathes through what is written.

Salvationists have no desire to live in the past, but we are ready to recognise the debt we owe to those who have gone before. We look to the future, under God, taking with us the sacred heritage he has given. These writings are part of that heritage. I hope and pray that this series will help and inspire all who use it, and that some will be prompted to contribute in written form to modern Salvationist literature in an age that needs also the old, eternal truths expressed in language for the 21st century.

The series is dedicated to the glory of God.

Shaw Clifton
General
London, July 2007

FOREWORD

What and Why We Believe is the latest book to be published in the 'Classic Salvationist Texts' series. It contains the text of two short books by one of The Salvation Army's most able thinkers and communicators, Lieut-Colonel Harry Dean – *The Faith We Declare* and *Belief in God*. First published in 1955 and 1961 respectively, both books competently explain Salvationist theology without recourse to theologians' language.

The Faith We Declare offers brief studies in Salvation Army doctrine, while *Belief in God* is a study in the Christian idea of the Godhead. Both utilise uncomplicated, day-to-day language which nevertheless stretches the mind of the reader in a healthy, helpful way.

What and Why We Believe will serve as a fitting memorial to Lieut-Colonel Dean, who died – in Salvation Army parlance was 'promoted to Glory – in June 2008 after a lifetime of distinguished service in literary and counselling work.

Charles King, Lieut-Colonel
Literary Secretary, International Headquarters
June 2009

BELIEF IN GOD

A study in the Christian idea
of the Godhead

Chapter One
THE BEING OF GOD

WHY write about someone you can't even see, who may not even exist at all? That's a fair question, so we must begin with that subject much-loved of the scientist, the subject of 'evidence'.

The existence of God
Imagine you have the opportunity of travelling the length and breadth of the world, from 'Greenland's icy mountains' to 'India's coral strand', what would you find? Among other things you would discover that, however countries and people differ one from another, everywhere gods of some kind are worshipped. Hindu worship differs from that of Islam, but that's to be expected. Within our Christian faith when you think how different a Quaker meeting is from one in The Salvation Army it's hardly surprising that different faiths find various means of expression. The point is that among all peoples there is an approach to the supernatural that is recognisable as worship, and such universality cannot be ignored.

Then again, supposing it was possible for us to look at a review of all past history, every picture would show signs of religion. The ancient writings of Egyptians and Babylonians – as well as the sacred books of the Jews that form our Old Testament – all bear witness to the same fact. The evidence from the caves in which prehistoric man dwelt points in the same direction. Throughout all time men and women have been questing for God.

Another fact is that it is futile to seek an explanation of all that exists in the material universe itself. Only the Unseen can explain the seen in any final way. The moving trees do not make the wind; it is the wind that causes the trees to move. The universe points beyond itself in two ways:

1. The question arises, why does the world exist at all?

Trace the chain of cause and effect back as far as you will, and behind all there must be a First Cause, an uncaused Cause. There is no alternative to this conclusion. In the last resort it must depend on a Being other than itself, and greater than itself. To reject such a belief means that our question remains unanswered.

2. The kind of world that exists points to a divine Creator.

There is design, order and beauty all around us which suggests a transcendent Designer. Man has penetrated many of nature's secrets and finds the world dependable, which suggests, among other things, that the Mind which made the world made also the mind of man.

A point of great importance, so often overlooked in certain agnostic circles, is that because a man has discovered 'how' some things may have happened he has not thereby accounted for the 'why' of those happenings. The province of the scientist is secondary causes, not ultimate issues.

Our knowledge of God

THE atheist, who denies the existence of God, has been described as a man with no invisible means of support. But how can we know anything about God in view of the fact that no one can see him? The New Testament states quite definitely: 'No one has ever seen God' (John 1:18).

Well, how do you get to know of people who live on the other side of the world? How does an American, for example, get to know the Japanese? In one of three ways (apart from actually making the journey to Japan):

1. He may see their work – what the Japanese worker produces in the way of such things as silks, cottons, toys.

2. He may receive messages from Japan – through books, letters, radio, television, films.

3. Some Japanese may actually visit him – and he will be able to see what they really are like.

Similarly, we get to know God through:

1. The things he has made (Psalm 19).

2. Those men and women who are specially sensitive to spiritual things and thus receive messages from God. This is why generations of Christians have turned to the Bible and found there divine truth.

3. The Lord Jesus Christ who, we believe, came to show us what God is like. To complete the verse of Scripture already quoted: 'God the One and Only, who is at the Father's side, has made him known.'

Even those who find themselves unable, or unwilling, to accept the full Christian gospel recognise the spiritual authority of Jesus Christ. What he taught about God is of the utmost importance and cannot be gainsaid by those who can hardly claim to be greater authorities! He declares that God is our Heavenly Father.

As a child he asks his parents: 'Didn't you know I had to be in my Father's house?' (Luke 2:49).

Teaching his disciples to pray, he says: 'When you pray, say: "Father"' (Luke 11:2).

Seeking to encourage the 12 apostles, he declares: 'Do not be afraid, little flock, for your Father has been pleased to give you the Kingdom' (Luke 12:32).

Promising spiritual power to his followers he states it is possible, 'because I am going to the Father' (John 14:12).

And praying from his Cross he cries: 'Father, into your hands I commit my spirit' (Luke 23:46).

Your earthly father may be many other things as well. He may be a doctor, or a teacher. In addition he may be a keen gardener, youth club leader and so on. But what matters to you most of all is that he is your father. In the same way, God is the Infinite, the Eternal and much besides, but you will get to know him best of all by thinking of him as your Heavenly Father.

Only one God

THE second doctrine of The Salvation Army reads:

We believe that there is only one God, who is infinitely perfect, the Creator, Preserver and Governor of all things, and who is the only proper object of religious worship.

In India, to take a present-day example, the majority of people believe in numerous gods. So did the ancient Greeks: there was a god of healing, a god of the sea, a god of war, and many others. In the Old Testament we read of the gods of the nations that surrounded Israel, called Baalim. The very days of the week are called after the names of gods that used to be worshipped – Sun, Moon, Tiw, Woden, Thor, Frig, Saturn.

Yet we believe in one God because of our conviction that Christianity is revelation in its completion. The references to other religions may lead someone to ask: 'Is it likely that one is true and all the rest are false? Does not such a view lead to a narrow fanaticism?' The answer is that the notion of 'one religion' and 'one God' is not itself narrow, but in harmony with a wide liberality of mind.

A scholar has written of the Lord Jesus: 'All religions find in him the perfect form of whatever truth they possess.' There is a finality about God's revelation in Christ which supersedes all other religions by including all the elements of truth which each contains in a more comprehensive whole. So the Buddhist or the Muslim can embrace Christianity and lose nothing; but the value of what he gains transcends all else.

Belief in many gods is belief in a multiplicity of causes, and this shows a lack of thoroughness in a person's thinking. As stated above, we must go back to the primary cause of all, to whom we give the name of 'God'.

That this conclusion is justified is confirmed by the fact that the universe is one great whole; the same laws apply throughout its vast distances, bearing witness to one Mind and purpose.

The nature of God
HE is the real and living God. One of the dangers of reading, writing or talking about God is that we could think of him as abstract. The Bible, where there are no vague definitions, never falls into this error. The God of Israel was the One 'who brought you out of the land of Egypt'. He was, and is, more than the Prime Mover; he was, and is, an active Agent in human affairs. He is the 'Creator, Preserver and Governor of all things'. A distinguished astronomer has stated that life would soon be impossible in the world unless hydrogen atoms were still being created. As a declared atheist, he presumably thinks they spring from no one out of nothing, where others see evidence of God's continued activity. But more than this, God hears our prayers and comes to our aid, and he can do this because he is the real and living God.

He is a good God. We find within the human heart an appreciation of goodness; in the presence of injustice and evil man rebels. Now man cannot be better than God, cannot have finer feelings than his Creator. Water, we say, cannot rise higher than its source, and man cannot elevate himself above God. Our conclusion must be that God is the Source of all that is finest in human nature; he is better than the best in man. All our thoughts of holiness have their origin in the One who is holy.

He is almighty. The presence of evil may seem to deny it, but actually it can form an argument in favour of this belief, although it may force us to rethink what we mean by 'power' and 'might'. Evil became a reality because God was mighty enough to give mankind its freedom and let that freedom work itself out in the world. That God has limited his own power is no argument against his almightiness. On the contrary, God demonstrates his power by making 'the wrath of man to praise him', by getting good out of evil, which is surely a much more difficult task than getting good out of good! There are, of course, some things that God cannot do; he cannot deny his own nature, which is love.

He is a loving God. Just as we need to rethink the word 'power' we must do the same with the word 'love'. We must not think of that strange state of mind and emotion called 'being in love'.

Love in the Bible is a steady direction of the will toward another's lasting good. Love means the coming to help in time of need; it means saving activity.

The proof of God's love is his 'saving activity' in the life, death and resurrection of Jesus. The depth, height and breadth of God's love could never be told – it could only be demonstrated. Thus he challenged men not with a word, but with the deed of the Cross.

He is Spirit. Here we are confronting a difficult idea. To say that God is Spirit may seem to suggest to some that he is unreal. Further thought should lead to the opposite conclusion, for spirit is more real than matter, or perhaps it would be truer to say that it is a higher order of reality. We recognise that the spirit of a person is more important than his body. If your father was involved in an accident and left with a crippled body, he would be just the same, just as loving and interested in you as before. The real person is not the body, which can be seen, but the self, which is unseen. The body is matter; the self is spirit. Very often the spirit within desires to do something which the body prevents, so spirit is a freer, higher kind of existence than matter. Now, just as the goodness in man points to a good Source, so spiritual existence points to a God who is Spirit (John 4:24).

He is everywhere. This follows from what has gone before. Matter can be in only one place at one time, but there are no such limitations for spirit. Even though our spirits are imprisoned in our bodies we can in thought and desire escape from the tyranny of space and roam the world. Then, in our dreams, we can escape to some extent the tyranny of time, and pass through all kinds of experiences in but a few seconds. God is limited by neither space nor time, but we should not think of God as being everywhere present like diffused gas may be in the atmosphere. Being Spirit he is in contact with spiritual personalities everywhere and at any time. Being love he seeks to be active in every circumstance of need. A human father may be too far away to hear the cry of his child, or may be unable to be with his children on occasions because duty demands his presence elsewhere. With God there are no such limitations; it cannot take any time for him to reach any place.

He is all-knowing. This, too, follows from the foregoing. A human father may have to say that he does not know because he was not there, or, though aware of certain circumstances, he cannot understand the meaning of what lies behind them. But a God who is everywhere is aware of all that transpires and, seeing he is the Creator, he cannot be baffled by anything that happens, even though much that takes place in his world is opposed to his own will. So, in regard to past and present, God is all-knowing, and he knows also all the possibilities of the future. This truth is both a challenge and a comfort.

In all our thinking about God we should remind ourselves that he is so much greater than our greatest ideas; we cannot hope fully to comprehend him. But, because he is Spirit and has made us in his likeness, we can know him for ourselves. To worship him is our chief duty and highest privilege.

Chapter Two
GOD MADE MANIFEST

JESUS CHRIST has been called 'the Man who broke history in two' because whenever we try to arrange what happened in the past we make his coming into the world the pivot – we say BC (Before Christ) and AD (Anno Domini, which means 'In the year of our Lord'). Every time we write the date on a letter we can recall that modern history begins from his birth. This is a recognition of his unique place in the story of man's life in the world.

'The Word became flesh'
WITHOUT Jesus Christ there would have been no Christianity, so to seek to understand him is of the utmost importance.

Many would be quite happy to regard him as the world's best Man, the finest religious teacher of all time, the greatest believer who lived. But that's not enough. Christians believe that in reaching Jesus they arrive at God, that he is himself the highest truth about the final Power of all, that he is God's personal response to man's basic need and therefore the answer to the piteous cry of the human heart. Jesus does not belong to the created, but is God become man. We read, 'the Word beame flesh' (see John 1:14).

Now a 'word' is an expressed 'thought'. Jesus Christ the 'Word' is the expression of the 'Thought' God, so that man can understand what otherwise would be unknown. But he is the 'Word' throughout all eternity. The wonderful truth over which we rejoice is that he 'became flesh'. He translated the meaning of 'God' into a human life, so that we see 'the glory of God in the face of Christ' (2 Corinthians 4:6).

Various attempts have been made to explain this great mystery, and at certain times Christian thinkers have laid so much emphasis on the humanity of Jesus that they have obscured his divinity and sometimes they have made the opposite mistake. The fourth doctrine of The Salvation Army seeks to safeguard us from either of these errors. It reads:

We believe that in the person of Jesus Christ the Divine and human natures are united, so that he is truly and properly God, and truly and properly man.

The humanity of Jesus Christ

JESUS was truly man; his humanity was no mere dress, appearance or pretence. We read of him being hungry, tired, surprised, indignant and so on. In the wilderness he was tempted, refusing to use his power to meet his own physical need (Matthew 4:1–11). Throughout his whole life, spiritual tests were coming to him. Of his disciples he said, 'You are those who have stood by me in my trials' ['temptations' *KJV*] (Luke 22:28). In the Epistle to the Hebrews we read, 'For we do not have a high priest who is unable to sympathise with our weaknesses, but we have one who has been tempted in every way, just as we are – yet was without sin' (4:15).

Then again, he suffered as other men suffer, in both body and mind. Finally, he died. And just as in the wilderness he refused to turn stones into bread so he refused to come down from the Cross. Having rejected even the drug that would have eased his pain, he would take no unworthy way out. He had committed himself to humanity 'for better, for worse'.

In *The Arabian Nights* the Caliph of Baghdad sometimes walked in disguise through the streets of the city, at night, to see how his people fared. But if at any time danger threatened he could immediately throw off the disguise and be the Caliph once more, with all his power and authority. Not so our Lord. His powers were at the disposal of the poor and needy, not at his own. Jesus knew that the divine nature did not consist of grasping, so he 'emptied himself', he 'dispossessed himself' (see Philippians 2:5–11).

> *They all were looking for a king*
> *To slay their foes and lift them high;*
> *Thou cam'st a little baby thing*
> *That made a woman cry.*
>   (George MacDonald).

Jesus was a real baby, then a real boy (he 'increased in wisdom and stature', Luke 2:52) and, finally, a real man. He lived a real life and died a real death, but there is so much more to be said!

The divinity of our Lord

FIRST, let's look at a surprising historic fact that no sceptic can deny. All of Jesus' first disciples were Jews and, as such, believers in one God. The experience of the nation during the exile in Babylon (the sixth century BC) had purged away any tendency to idolatry, and for centuries the descendants of those who returned to Palestine maintained a remarkable expression of pure religion. The first two commandments ('You shall have no other gods before me' and 'You shall not make for yourself an idol in the form of anything in heaven above or on the earth beneath or in the waters below') expressly forbade idolatry in any form. At that time the pure monotheism (belief in one God) of the Jewish nation was the envy of innumerable high-minded Gentiles. Yet it was a group of people from this nation who began to worship Jesus Christ, with whom they had actually lived. They gave him the name that had been used for Jehovah in their sacred writings.

Turn to the New Testament. The men and women there are not looking back on Jesus, remembering him as human; they are looking up to him, revering him as divine. Mark's Gospel – probably the first to be written, therefore reflecting the thought of believers at a very early stage – provides an example. (Try to read it through at a sitting;

if you are a medium-paced reader it will take you 40 minutes.) The humanity of Jesus stands out clearly, but it is not a purely human story. Jesus had the power to read men's minds and hearts and to forgive their sins; he said he would rise from the dead and is presented as the destined judge of mankind.

Then in the Acts of the Apostles you will discover that from the very beginning the early Church saw in the death of Jesus the love of God.

And what was true for those first-century Christians has been true for all succeeding centuries. Whenever men who know about Jesus Christ worship God, they find his figure intercepting their gaze and mediating their homage. And the sincere seeker who hears of him for the first time often responds, 'I knew there ought to be a God like that.'

Jesus has become the test of the Divine in human experience. However the world may fail to follow him, the world will never now believe in any lesser God than he stands for. He is the limit of our seeing Godward. His Deity is effective. He is our category for God.

Now is this all delusion, the greatest confidence-trick in history? Either those early disciples were led into blasphemous idolatry by the One whom all men (believers, agnostics and even atheists) recognise as a great moral teacher, or they discovered the amazing truth. Either 19 centuries of Christian believers – including many of the most acute minds – have been misled, or the staggering claim we make for Jesus Christ is valid. But make sure you understand the position. If you decide that the disciples were wrong and the continuing Christian Church is likewise deluded, you cannot retain Jesus as an example and guide in any sense, because you will have concluded that he was the world's greatest deceiver.

This short book cannot deal in any full way with such a large question, but before leaving this part of the subject, consider briefly two facts about our Lord.

Firstly, he was as intimate with God as we are with our parents. He spoke so naturally of his 'Father'. Most descriptions of God are like the essays of schoolchildren on great men they have only read about, but Jesus undoubtedly knew his Father in the most intimate of ways. He said, 'I am in the Father and the Father is in me' (John 14:11) and spoke of death itself as simply a journey to the Heavenly Father's home (John 14:1–12). Note, too, that in spite of his utter humility, Jesus referred to his own Sonship as something different from ours (Matthew 11:27).

Secondly, Jesus lived a sinless life. He yielded to no temptation, and nothing that men did to him could make him cease loving them, for he prayed even for his murderers (Luke 23:34). He could challenge his enemies, 'Can any of you prove me guilty of sin?' (John 8:46), and finally they only succeeded in condemning him by bribing men to bear false witness (Matthew 26:59, 60). Both Pilate and the centurion at the Cross declared him innocent.

Now the better a person is, the more aware he becomes of failure and sin, and yet Jesus, whose goodness friends and foes alike acclaim, was aware of no shortcoming. Such sinlessness sets him apart from the rest of mankind. How can we account for it? From whatever angle we approach him it becomes necessary to regard him as divine.

The Saviour of the world
JESUS came to reveal what God is like. We believe that God 'has been unfolded by the divine One, the only Son' (John 1:18 *Moffatt Translation*). Not that we imagine that because of him we know everything about God, for that, obviously, is beyond us. He did not come to demonstrate what we call God's 'attributes', such as omnipotence, omnipresence or omniscience. He came to disclose character; to show what God is like in himself, not all the things God can do. Not the powers of God, but his nature is what matters to man in his weakness and shame.

This leads us to the truth that Jesus did more than reveal God; he came to redeem man. He stands before us not only as example and guide, but as Saviour and Lord.

The whole of the Incarnation was sacrificial. God, in Jesus, entered our confined world. It has been said that 'the genius of parenthood lies in achieving a real common life with your child'. The adult must come down to the child's real experience of life, and if this is achieved the child finds in his parent's understanding and contact his own salvation.

In Jesus, God has been passing 'the low lintel of the human heart'. There was the limitation of the body, the weakness of babyhood, the poverty and labour of a peasant's workshop, the experience of temptation, the insults of ignorant men, the misunderstanding of friends and relatives, the rejection by his own nation, the death of a slave on a Roman cross.

His death was his life in its final outcome. It demonstrated, as nothing else could have done, the sacrificial love to which the whole of his life bore witness. And his suffering on behalf of, and at the hands of men was God's way of saving the world. It was divine love bearing human sin, and bearing it away. It was divine weakness triumphing over the strength of evil, and making personal victory possible for all who will believe.

For Jesus' death was not the end. We enter a graveyard and read 'Here lies ...', but those who visited the place of Jesus' burial were greeted by a very different message – 'He is risen'. Had his death been the end of the story the whole moral and spiritual world would have been shattered. Men would have been forced to abandon their faith in a loving and righteous God, for hate would have triumphed over love, evil over good.

Because of his victory, there is hope for all men. Jesus Christ is the world's Saviour. He saves from despair and from sin. His life and death are the pledge of God's love and the offer of God's forgiveness and grace.

The Lord of life

JESUS rose from the dead, and because of this he has never been a dead issue in the affairs of men. Always he has to be reckoned with, and ultimately his will be the last word.

A handful of Galileans, mostly fishermen, and all from the ordinary walks of life, began a movement – under the inspiration of the Holy Spirit – that soon conquered the Roman Empire. Jesus had returned to the 'right hand of God' (the language is symbolic) from where he was influencing and changing men and human history. 'Christ ... is not weak in dealing with you, but is powerful among you' (2 Corinthians 13:3).

Tradition tells us that in the fourth century AD, Julian, the Roman Emperor, cried out, 'Thou hast conquered, O pale Galilean.' Henrick Ibsen in *Emperor and Galilean* made him continue: 'Where is he now? What if he goes on and on . . . conquers again from world to world?' Is not this what he has been doing? From the eternal world he still makes his impact on this world and its affairs.

When he first the work begun,
Small and feeble was his day:
Now the word doth swiftly run,
Now it wins its widening way;
More and more it spreads and grows,
Ever mighty to prevail;
Sin's strongholds it now o'erthrows,
Shakes the trembling gates of Hell.
(*Charles Wesley, SASB 165*)

The now famous saying of Charles Lamb always will be true: 'If Shakespeare were to come into this room we should all rise to our feet. But if that Person were to enter we should kneel and try to kiss the hem of his garment.'

The wonder of wonders is that he is always in this room, wherever that may be. He is near to every needy heart, 'the same yesterday, and today, and for ever' (Hebrews 13:8).

We can with confidence look forward to the day when

Jesus shall reign where'er the sun
Doth his successive journeys run;
His kingdom stretch from shore to shore,
Till suns shall rise and set no more.
(*Isaac Watts, SASB 160*)

In the New Testament we read:

'Therefore God exalted him to the highest place and gave him the name that is above every name, that at the name of Jesus every knee should bow, in heaven and on earth and under the earth, and every tongue confess that Jesus Christ is Lord, to the glory of God the Father' (Philippians 2:9-11).

Our great responsibility and privilege is to labour and pray for the day of Christ's completed mission.

Chapter Three
GOD IN MAN

HAVE you ever seen a person in love? He or she appears to be walking on air, and in the eye has appeared a new light. Have you ever seen someone in a rage? He – it's bound to be 'he' this time! – may be left almost speechless, and it is a fire, rather than a light, that burns in the eye. Or perhaps you yourself have felt tremendously excited about something. Unable to eat, concentrate, or do anything worthwhile, your feelings have bubbled up within you and become well nigh uncontrollable. Of people in love, or in a temper, or in a state of excitement, we sometimes say they act as though they are 'possessed'.

That's just what the onlookers thought about Peter and the rest of the disciples on the day of Pentecost (read the thrilling story in the second chapter of Acts). In fact, some went so far as to say they were drunk, but Peter – with marked lucidity – explained that they were in fact 'possessed'. God's Holy Spirit (sometimes called the Holy Ghost) had been poured out upon them as had been promised.

Before we are able to understand the meaning of that wonderful, if strange, happening, we shall need to look farther back still.

Was not the Holy Spirit at work in Old Testament times? Surely, too, he was operative in the life of Jesus? What did Jesus have to say about him? These are the questions we need to face before coming to grips with the significance of Pentecost.

The Spirit in the Old Testament
FROM the earliest times, the Hebrews had spoken of certain happenings as the result of the activity of the Spirit of Jehovah. This

was the case even with such things as great physical strength. When we read of Samson tearing apart a young lion the explanation is given that 'the Spirit of the Lord came upon him in power' (Judges 14:5, 6). In Exodus 31:2, 3 we learn of the carving and engraving of the Tabernacle by Bezaleel, and his artistic skill was because God had granted him his own Spirit 'with skill, ability and knowledge, in all kinds of crafts'. In an early story of the wilderness wanderings we are told that Moses selected 70 elders who prophesied when the Spirit came upon them (Numbers 11:25).

Also in those far-off days the Spirit was active transforming individuals. As a preparation for the kingship of Israel, Saul was told 'the Spirit of the Lord will come upon you in power ... and you will be changed into a different person'. Later on, when Saul had failed, we read that 'the Spirit of the Lord had departed from Saul' and 'from that day on the Spirit of the Lord came upon David in power' (I Samuel 10:6; 16:14, 13).

Then again, in the later books of the Old Testament other ideas begin to find expression. For instance, in Isaiah 11 we have the picture of the Ideal King, and the very first thing that is said about him is: 'the Spirit of the Lord will rest on him' endowing him with all the qualities of the Perfect Ruler. Of his 'Servant' (in the later chapters of Isaiah) God is represented as saying, 'I will put my Spirit on him' (42:1). It will also spring to mind that when Jesus began his public ministry at Nazareth he claimed that the prophecy found in Isaiah (61:1, 'the Spirit of the Lord is on me') was fulfilled in himself.

Jesus and the Holy Spirit
IN the story of Jesus' baptism (Mark 1:9-11) we read: 'As Jesus was coming up out of the water, he saw heaven being torn open and the Spirit descending on him like a dove.' Here we have an interesting contrast: the Hebrew word used for the coming of the Spirit in the Old Testament suggests a violent breaking in upon a man, like an axe cleaving the resistant wood; but the Spirit came to the receptive will and mind of Jesus 'like a dove'. This event was the divine equipment

for the tasks ahead. The Holy Spirit, associated with his birth (Luke 1:35), was his in full measure.

When his death drew near Jesus told the disciples that his departure was 'for their good' (John 16:7). How difficult it must have been for them to believe that! How could Jesus' death be a good thing in any way? To think of it as a gain for themselves was impossible. And yet it was so, because his 'going' was the prelude to the Spirit's 'coming'.

In the later chapters of John's Gospel we have much of Jesus' teaching on this important subject. First and foremost, the Spirit is the Teacher and Witness of Christ. Two statements of our Lord are fundamental to our understanding. They are John 14:26 and 16:14. Make sure you read and grasp their meaning. The function of the Spirit is not to speak of himself, but of Christ. He makes real in the heart of the believer the presence of Jesus. We will return to this.

In addition, Jesus taught that the Spirit is in the world convicting men of sin and bringing about their repentance: he works upon men's consciences making them see the need for righteous living (John 16:8); he guides into all truth (John 16:13), and is the *Paraklètos* (John 14:26). This last word is translated 'Counsellor', but its real meaning is perhaps better suggested by the term 'Advocate'. Literally it means 'someone called alongside to help', indeed a very comforting truth and experience.

The promise fulfilled

WE can now return to the second chapter of 'Acts'. This happening brought into existence the Christian Church.

Great spiritual experiences are always very difficult to describe; but how graphic are the words used! We must not allow, however, the temporary and passing signs (the sound like a violent wind from heaven, the tongues of fire resting on them, or the speaking in other tongues) to cause us to forget the main point. Jesus' promise was being fulfilled. Sometimes we may be tempted to think that if we lead a life of honesty and self-control we are Christians, that if we possess a kindly disposition we have the Spirit of Christ, but Pentecost means that new energies and a new love are necessary, and these new possibilities are open to all.

Now what had happened to the disciples? Fear had caused them to forsake their Lord in the garden of Gethsemane; Peter had disowned him; thereafter they met behind closed doors. But here we see them out in the open, speaking in Jesus' name, accusing the leaders of the nation as the murderers of the Messiah of God, showing a courage that was not their own. This was all because the Holy Spirit brought a vivid awareness of their Master's living presence. It was the Spirit of Jesus who had returned to them in power, as an inner vital principle of their lives.

The coming of Jesus might be described as 'out of the everywhere (eternity) into the here (time)'. The ascension of Jesus (Acts 1:1–11) reversed this process: he went 'out of the here' back 'into the everywhere'. Had nothing altered then? Would everything be 'as you were'? Far from it. The Holy Spirit, who had been active in olden times and in the life of Jesus, could now operate in a new way. He had a new vehicle of expression; the coming, the life, the deeds, the teaching, the death and resurrection of the Lord Jesus Christ could now be spread abroad throughout the whole wide world. What had been 'local' in Jesus could now become 'universal'. What happened in Palestine could now exercise effective action in Poland or Peru. And ever since that day the work of the Holy Spirit has been to let people know that Jesus is available as Saviour and Sanctifier to all the centuries and to all the world.

This is what has been happening ever since.

He (the Holy Spirit) speaks to Luther and produces the Reformation; to Wycliffe and Tyndale, and the Bible is translated into English; to Wesley, and the Church is led into a new life when it has been cold and dead; to Raikes, and Sunday-schools spring up all over the land; to Shaftesbury, and there is a new sense of social righteousness.

The list, indeed, is endless. Cannot we say with truth that the Spirit spoke to William and Catherine Booth, and The Salvation Army was born?

He is still active. This very day he may urge a Christian poet to write a song of praise that will help millions, or guide a scientist to a discovery that will bless the world, or prompt a politician to put forward legislation to benefit mankind. And all this is because the Holy Spirit can now use the revelation of God in Jesus which has life and power and meaning for every situation and all time.

The Holy Spirit and ourselves
JOHN Wesley described his conversion experience by saying, ' I felt my heart strangely warmed, and knew . . . .' This happy feeling, and blessed knowledge is sometimes called the 'assurance' or witness of the Spirit. In this way we realise that we are right with God. In point of fact, of course, the whole process which led up to the critical experience of conversion, and the experience itself, was part of the Holy Spirit's activity.

The Spirit makes men holy. How could it be otherwise? The forgiveness of God for past evil must become the springboard of moral and spiritual action, begun and sustained by the Spirit, leading on to real goodness. He does this in two ways: firstly, by cleansing the heart of bad desires; secondly, by creating good desires in their place, more and more filling the heart with love for God and men.

Then he helps us in our prayer-life, by teaching us the things for which we should ask and – more wonderful still – himself asking on our behalf, for 'we do not know what we ought to pray for' (Romans 8:26). He leads us into the truth of Christ, enlightening mind and heart by Jesus' idea of goodness, and helping us to understand and apply the Bible to our personal lives. Then, having revealed what is right, he gives the power to achieve. The fact that the Holy Spirit speaks of Jesus, not of himself, is of the greatest practical aid, for we can easily test ourselves to see to what extent we are Spirit-filled. The question 'Is Jesus becoming increasingly real?' provides a sure guide.

Read Galatians 5:22, 23 for Paul's list of the 'fruit of the Spirit'. Sometimes we are tempted to think that the evidence of the Spirit's presence is in exciting happenings and deep emotional stirrings. Without belittling anything of this nature, it is good to note that Paul lists the quiet virtues of love, longsuffering, gentleness and meekness. These are the signs of the Spirit's indwelling, and if we lack them we should be driven to examine ourselves with great care and honesty. Think of each virtue in turn, and ask, 'How much ... is there in any life? Can I give myself 50 or 60 – or only 15 – out of 100 for love, joy, temperance ... ?

Perhaps a word of caution might not be out of place here. We speak of the Spirit coming 'down', or 'filling' the heart. These are spatial terms that we cannot help using, but we should recognise them for what they are. The Holy Spirit does not occupy space in this way, for here we are thinking of another realm of existence altogether. It may help us to think of those people who have certain mental links with each other; for example, identical twins. Though separated by many miles the sickness of one may disturb the other, or the decision of 'A' in New York may affect 'B' in London. This is all very mysterious, but no one imagines that anything actually passes from the one to the other, nothing crosses the Atlantic which separates 'A' from 'B'. This is because we are in the realm of the mind, not matter; space does not enter into the situation. So it is in the spiritual world. There is no need for the Holy Spirit to move from here to there. He has links with us of quite a different order, and wherever there is spiritual need He is present.

Holy Spirit, truth divine,
Dawn upon this soul of mine;
Word of God and inward light,
Wake my spirit, clear my sight.

Holy Spirit, love divine,
Glow within this heart of mine;
Kindle every high desire,
Perish self in thy pure fire.
(Samuel Longfellow, SASB 194)

The Trinity

GOD the Father, God the Son, and God the Holy Spirit, are the three 'Persons' of the Trinity of whom our third doctrine affirms that they are 'undivided in essence and co-equal in power and glory'. A somewhat bewildering doctrine this.

All essential doctrine flows out of human experience, as did this one. The Hebrews rejected the polytheism (belief in many gods) of their neighbours; the early disciples, who believed in 'one God', found themselves worshipping Jesus as divine; the early Church was overwhelmed with a sense of the Holy Spirit's presence, making Jesus real. Confronted with these three historic facts, believers formulated the doctrine of the 'Tri-unity' of God; he is the 'Three-in-One'. Because of it we can worship God the Father, Jesus the Son, and the Holy Spirit, as divine, while still believing in one God. 'But', someone may ask impatiently, 'how can three be one, and one be three? Aren't you playing about with words?'

All attempts to illustrate or explain this profound truth are bound to fall short somewhere, but we do know of other 'trinities'. Man consists of body, mind and spirit, and our personalities are made up of thought, feeling and will. It might help to think of Her Majesty, Queen Elizabeth the Second. She is a woman, a Queen, and a mother. Sometimes she speaks as a woman (about what she likes and does not like), sometimes as a Queen (on all official occasions), and sometimes as mother (when addressing her children). Then again, as a woman she is entitled to her children's respect, as a Queen, to their allegiance, and as a mother she calls forth their love. The illustration is imperfect, but there is a sense in which Her Majesty is three persons in one.

These are but hints and nothing more. That a full understanding of God is beyond our powers is not surprising. There is only one God, but we know him in three ways – God the absolute (the Father), God the self-revealing (the Son), and God the self-imparting (the Spirit). Each plays a part in our salvation and in the whole life of faith. Whenever we approach God we pray to the Father, in the name of the Son, by the aid of the Spirit.

The Christian idea of the Godhead is relevant to everyday life. Our great need is an awareness of the spiritual dimension in which our lives are set. It is certain that in this life we can never expect fully to comprehend God; but it is also certain that without God we can never expect properly to understand anything else. Einstein used to say that although God is intricate he is not deceitful. Having known the love of God in Christ, we can trust him utterly and, through the Holy Spirit, find that love shed abroad in our own hearts.

Belief in the Fatherhood of God requires that we live as his children, showing the family likeness. Belief in the Saviourhood of Christ demands the response of daily, open-hearted obedience. Belief in the power and presence of the Holy Spirit must produce a harvest of love and joy and peace. What we believe must become part of life itself.

THE FAITH WE DECLARE

Brief Studies in Salvation Army Doctrine

INTRODUCTION

NO STUDY of Christian doctrine should be followed without an understanding of the limitations of doctrine as such. Doctrines are formulations of truth, the means by which we believe. They form a kind of telescope through which we seek to see meanings, and we must not confuse the telescope with the vision that it may clarify. The truth is personal; it is Jesus Christ. A person may possess him and yet hold certain erroneous views regarding various aspects of Christian doctrine. On the other hand, a person may hold all the correct views – be perfectly orthodox – and yet be far removed from the truth.

Our 'beliefs', then, need to be seen as related to but different from our 'faith'. Faith is not the holding of correct doctrines, but personal fellowship with God in Christ. William Temple wrote:

Correct doctrine will both express this, assist it and issue from it; incorrect doctrine will misrepresent this and hinder or prevent it. Doctrine is of an importance too great to be exaggerated, but its place is secondary not primary. I do not believe in any creed, but I use certain creeds to express, to conserve, and to deepen my faith in God. What is offered to man's apprehension in any specific revelation is not truth concerning God, but the living God himself.

Doctrine, then, is not faith. Faith is a committal of oneself to the Lord Jesus, and thereafter it is a constant quest, an 'adult occupation of the mind'.

Chapter One

THE BIBLE

1. *We believe that the Scriptures of the Old and New Testaments were given by inspiration of God; and that they only constitute the Divine rule of Christian faith and practice.*

THESE studies deal with the 11 points of doctrine set forth in The Salvation Army's Foundation Deed. The Army belongs to the main line of Christian tradition, holding the orthodox Christian faith, so our first doctrine relates to the Bible.

The supreme value of the Bible to us lies in the simple fact that it brings Jesus Christ out of the past into the present, out of history right into the 21st century. We love and worship the Lord Jesus, but the references made to him by secular historians are of little value or consequence. Without the Bible we should be bereft of that knowledge of Christ which we believe is essential to our salvation. Wycliffe's irrefutable contention was: 'To be ignorant of the Scriptures is to be ignorant of Christ.'

The one theme of the whole Bible is *the loving and redeeming purpose of God*. In the Old Testament we read how God chose the Hebrews to be the vehicle of his truth. At each historical crisis prophets arose to relate that crisis to God's purpose, and here we have the record of those inspired moments in this people's history. The revelation contained in the Old Testament is necessarily a progressive one, and the ever-increasing light brought ever-increasing responsibility. Alas, to see the truth is not always to do it, and the Hebrews often grievously failed to be true to the highest insights of their own inspired men.

Throughout human history God has ever been seeking to reveal himself to mankind, to break through into human understanding and, by doing so, to enter the lives and experiences of individual men and women. In the Old Testament we have the fascinating story of how God was doing this 'at many times and in various ways' (Hebrews 1:1).

The Old Testament, however, is but a partial revelation. There is a climax and a culmination. Martin Luther truly described the Bible as 'the crib where Christ is laid'. The Old Testament is a preparation for him; the Gospels give us the story of his birth, life, death and resurrection; the Acts of the Apostles tells of the impact upon the Roman Empire of the small group of his disciples through the power of the Holy Spirit; from the Epistles that follow we gather something of the teaching of the Early Church, his Church; and the whole is brought to a magnificent conclusion by the Revelation of John, which foretells his final triumph.

There can be no authority beyond truth, and truth is not a visible or tangible thing unless God himself, who is Truth, becomes man. This miracle is what the Bible affirms. Christ is God's Word and therein lies his authority. He is authority.

God spoke *through* the Old Testament prophets, but he spoke *in* his Son. The word of God *came* to such as Amos, Hosea and Jeremiah, but when Jesus entered history the 'Word became flesh' – no longer a 'spelled-out' word, but *a 'lived-out' Word*. There are some things that words cannot say, or, even if they could be said, they need not be believed, but in all things Christ not only spoke the truth of God, he *demonstrated* that truth in a way that cannot be disputed. Truly he has 'led God forth into full revelation'.

Ignatius said: 'My authentic records are Jesus Christ, his Cross and his resurrection.' The Bible is essential as an 'historical credential', an introduction to Christ, the living Word. 'The living impress of Christ on hearts of men in his day becomes again the living impress on ours.' In this way the Bible is more than the record of a past revelation that is dead; it is the medium of a present revelation that is alive. It is, we believe, God's appointed way of entering into communication with men of every age.

The purpose of revelation is nothing less than the gift of the life of God to the life of man. Man's need is not scientific, so the purpose of divine revelation is not to give man knowledge of the physical universe which he can discover for himself. *Man's need is spiritual*, hence in the Bible we find those spiritual truths which man must understand if he is to find his right place as a spiritual personality in this material universe. Man's greatest need, whether or not he recognises it, is redemption, and here we have the record of all that God has done to meet that need.

It is not enough to read the Bible as great literature, which, of course, it is. The man who reads it with a vital sense of shortcoming discovers the light by which he can find his way. The self-sufficient man may not find it speaking to his heart, although there have been amazing instances of how God has used the written word to penetrate and expose a man's inner life, enabling him to read the small print of his own soul, and then to find the stern comfort of pardon through penitence.

Finally, it is important to realise that 'authority' and 'truth' have to be *perceived*. To say that one cannot 'see anything in the Bible' is not an indictment on the Bible, but on oneself. Ultimately there is no such thing as external authority for the soul. Jesus, when asked about his authority, gave no direct answer (Matthew 21: 23–27), but asked his questioners to tell him of the authority of John the Baptist, the inference being that if they had failed to perceive the Baptist's authority, they could not be expected to understand his. Moral and spiritual authority cannot be claimed, it can only be recognised. In this way Salvationists recognise the authority of the Bible.

Chapter Two
BELIEF IN GOD

2. *We believe that there is only one God, who is infinitely perfect, the Creator Preserver and Governor of all things, and who is the only proper object of religious worship.*

A FAMOUS writer used to say that when renting rooms, he did not ask the landlady about trivial things, such as how much per week and whether it included laundry, but inquired about her philosophy of life! The most important thing is, of course, our total view of life: whether or not we believe in God who has a purpose of love for mankind. Man can live fully and happily with many of his intellectual problems unsolved, but he cannot do so with a moral and spiritual inexplicability at the heart of his universe.

There are three main attitudes to this fundamental question: that of the atheist, who denies the existence of any intelligent purpose whatever; the agnostic, who, in theory, suspends judgment; the believer, who says, 'I believe in God'.

Let it be admitted that life is a maze. To the atheist the maze has no centre – a truly terrifying thought. He will not concede that the unseen exists; life is matter variously arranged, and mind is nothing more than the by-product of the brain. He has been described aptly as one who has no invisible means of support!

The agnostic does not specifically deny purpose in creation. He claims that while there *may* be a centre to the maze of life, it is both unknown and unknowable; a most depressing conclusion. Pitchforked into life without a clue, we are not going to be allowed to find one. Strange to say, many agnostics spend a good deal of time speculating on the nature of what cannot be known! They usually think in impersonal terms, which is in itself a denial of their boasted attitude of 'suspended judgment'. A true agnostic should at least admit the possibility that the Christian may be right, for he himself is 'a witness that testifies to nothing' and therefore should be ignored.

The Salvationist, as a believer, rejects the views of both atheist and agnostic. To the atheist he declares that it is futile to seek an explanation of all things in the material universe which points beyond itself. Only the Unseen can finally explain the seen. It is easy to show that the atheistic conclusion really invalidates the reasoning leading to that conclusion. If there is no purpose in life, there is no purpose that created the atheist's mind. Why then does he trust his own reasoning? It is necessary to believe in a purposeful creation (some kind of 'God') in order to accept one's reasoning powers as being in any way reliable. To trust one's thought processes is an act of sheer, if necessary, faith. To quote Augustine: 'Not all who believe think, but he who thinks believes. He believes in thinking.'

As a believer, the Salvationist points out that the agnostic's attitude is but a pose, for on ultimate issues it is not possible to suspend judgment. Agnosticism moves over into the attitude of denial, and is therefore little different from atheism. It is essentially impracticable. Man either acts as if he believes in God, or as if he does not believe; he either prays, or he does not pray; he either follows Christ, or does not follow Christ. As Jesus himself said: 'He who is not with me is against me, and he who does not gather with me scatters' (Matthew 12:30). *There can be no middle course.* The practical necessity of living, forces man to declare himself as for or against. Salvationists declare themselves quite definitely 'for'.

Thomas Hardy, one of the greatest of English novelists, was an agnostic, but he thought of God as a 'vast imbecility'. Now to deny that there is sanity at the heart of things is not agnosticism at all. Where was his 'suspended judgment'? His real position was atheistic. Further, if he had driven his definition to its logical conclusion, he would have had the humiliation of admitting that he himself was the creation of an imbecile!

Hardy, I am confident, would have protested his own sanity. Where, then, did that sanity come from? Was Hardy, who presumed to criticise the universe in which he found himself, greater than his own Creator? Endeavouring to show the inadequacy of other views is more than a negative way of stating the case for belief in the Christian's conception of God; it has positive value. Professor John Baillie, of Edinburgh University, stated that many of his friends had returned to the full Christian outlook by 'awakening to the essential untenability of the alternative positions. ... Their apostasy needed only to become robustly self-critical in order to lose all its conviction.'

There is certainly much that challenges the Christian's faith in God, but there is more that challenges unbelief. For the believer there is the problem of evil, but for the unbeliever there is the problem of goodness. How can goodness exist in a Godless world? How would we know anything was good or bad? As one of John Galsworthy's characters says: 'Why is decency the decent thing if there is no God?'

Chapter Three
THE TRINITY

3. *We believe that there are three persons in the Godhead – the Father, the Son and the Holy Ghost, undivided in essence and co-equal in power and glory.*

HERE we are in the presence of mystery, but it would be folly to repudiate the idea expressed in this statement because of that fact. It is good to remember that there are mysteries in other realms. T. H. Huxley, the great agnostic of the last century, once declared: 'The mysteries of the Church are child's play compared with the mysteries of nature – the Trinity is not more puzzling than the contradictions of natural science.'

Life would be a poor thing if everything was as plain and lucid as the multiplication table, for there is a mystery that does not annul meaning, but enriches it. Salvationists believe that the Christian doctrine of the Trinity is a mystery of light, not of darkness.

Personality, as we know it in ourselves and in others, involves distinction and separateness, and naturally it is difficult for us to conceive of it apart from this exclusiveness. Yet there is no reason why we should jump to the conclusion that exclusive individuality is *necessary* to personality. This is why it is better to say: 'God is personal', rather than say: 'God is *a* Person' for the indefinite article suggests this particularity and exclusiveness which we must try to transcend. In the same way, the saying of Jesus is rendered as 'God is Spirit', not 'God is *a* Spirit' (John 4:24).

In order to refute all *im*personal conceptions of God, Christians must maintain that God is personal, but we should not assume that personality in God needs to be identical with personality in man or suffers from any limitation whatever. Surely it is reasonable to suggest that the essence and nature of God must lie beyond our present understanding, for a God fully understood by man would be no God at all.

It is important to observe that this doctrine is not a piece of gratuitous speculation which theologians have tacked on to the gospel. It grew up out of sheer historic necessity.

First of all there was the monotheism that was the living heart of Old Testament religion. 'Hear, O Israel: The Lord our God, the Lord is one' (Deuteronomy 6:4).

Secondly, the early disciples, monotheists in heart and practice, found themselves worshipping Jesus as God.

Thirdly, in the Early Church there was an overwhelming sense of the Holy Spirit's presence, making Jesus real. The revelation of Christ had become a creative, continuous, life-giving experience for all believers.

The Christian Church, confronted with these three facts, and seeing the need to guard the essentials of its faith, formulated the doctrine of the Trinity. The doctrine flowed out of history and experience, and is intended to preserve the right to offer worship to Jesus Christ and the Holy Spirit as divine, while retaining unimpaired the belief that there is only one God.

All attempts to illustrate this profound truth are bound to be inadequate, if not misleading, and perhaps for the best treatment we need to go back to Augustine. He started from the fact that God is love. Now the verb 'to love' is what grammarians call a transitive verb. For love to be a reality at all there need to be *three* realities: one who loves, one who is loved, and the love itself. If, then, it is an eternal truth that 'God is love', from all eternity there must have been *in* God *a Lover, a Loved One* and *Love*. It is pointless to try to argue that the Lover must have preceded either the Loved One or the Love. This is only necessary *in our thinking*; it is neither necessary, nor indeed possible, in fact.

The conclusion is this: the Father loves the Son, and the Holy Spirit is the Spirit of Love which unites Father and Son. It is obvious that love is a social activity and cannot exist in isolation. Therefore it becomes necessary for us to conceive of God as a 'divine society'.

Chapter Four
JESUS, HUMAN AND DIVINE

4. *We believe that in the person of Jesus Christ the Divine and human natures are united; so that he is truly and properly God; and truly and properly man.*

COMMON sense might urge that Jesus must be either human or divine, and once again we have to admit that here we are in the presence of mystery and need to beware of a desire for over-simplification. In our impatience with paradox and our desire for a too common-sense theology we may lose something of vital importance. T. S. Eliot has said: 'A heresy is apt to have a seductive simplicity ... and to be altogether more plausible than the truth.'

We must not be led astray by those who would suggest that such ideas as are expressed in this doctrine were a later imposition upon a much simpler gospel. The truth is that from the very beginning Christianity had a theology. The early Christians did not gather together to admire a remarkable teacher of prophetic genius, but to worship a risen, ascended and living Lord, ascribing to him the very name used for 'Jehovah' in their sacred writings, which we now call the 'Old Testament'.

The men and women of the New Testament are not looking *back* on Jesus, remembering him as human; they are looking *up* to him, revering him as divine. Examine Mark's Gospel as an example (and this is generally recognised as the first of our four Gospels to have been written); the humanity of Jesus stands out very clearly – he was hungry, tired, surprised, grieved and indignant. But it is not a purely human story – he had power to read men's minds and hearts and to forgive their sins; he said he would rise from the dead and is presented as the destined Judge of mankind.

So, in seeking to understand the Incarnation, Salvationists are aware that they face a problem that cannot be explained with absolute lucidity. The coming of Jesus was 'an historical event *plu*s'. It was a mighty act of God. Jesus came *into* history, not *out* of it. He was no mere product of humanity, for in him the Eternal crossed into the temporal. Jesus is God's ideal for man, and for man – the image of God.

Close study of the four Gospels reveals the complete God-consciousness of Jesus. In all the human decisions and choices he made, he discounted his own personal contribution, and gave the glory to God. It has been truly said, 'the God-Man is the only man who claims nothing for himself, but all for God'. So Paul could declare: '*God* was *in* Christ' (2 Corinthians 5:19, *NKJV*).

Approached from this standpoint one of the most perplexing incidents in the Gospel narrative, the conversation between Jesus and the rich young ruler, becomes very illuminating. Hailed by the young man as 'Good teacher', Jesus responded, 'Why do you call me good? No-one is good except God alone' (Mark 10:18). This reply does not reveal self-deprecation on the part of Jesus for, as seen in the Sermon on the Mount with his '*I say unto you*', he was aware of his own spiritual authority. Jesus was concerned lest the young man should fail to relate the goodness he recognised to God, the Source of all goodness. He was so conscious of God that he was not conscious of possessing goodness himself, independent of God. Thus 'our Lord's moral perfection includes human humility'. So, dominated by a sense of God, he sought to turn the young seeker's eyes towards his Heavenly Father.

In this way he translated the abstract truth about God into a real human life so that there men might find the answer to the suffocating doubt that sometimes almost overwhelms the sincere seeker after reality. There may be many aspects of God which are totally beyond the range of finite human intelligence, but all that man is capable of understanding, Jesus reveals.

Is it not strange how men instinctively feel that the life of Jesus is quite unique? No one ever asks why he was not a better man. At Easter-time we listen to the gospel song 'Were you there when they crucified my Lord?' and nobody appears to think the question ridiculous. Why is this? Is it not because something within us, deeper than reason, recognises that in the death of Jesus we have something more than an isolated event in human history? That just as the volcanic eruption reveals momentarily the fires that are ever burning beneath the crust of the earth, so the Cross reveals the eternal truth about God? God always has been, and always will be, what Jesus declared by his life, teaching and death.

Some thinking people are offended by such a message as this. The whole idea of God becoming man is, in their view, fantastic – imagination run riot. They would go so far as to deny the very existence of Jesus, rather than give countenance to the miracle of his life, although the historicity of Jesus is one of the best attested facts in the ancient world. But it is the thief who prospers in the darkness, and it is the materialist who requires that there should be no Christ.

Let us face a final question: can we really believe that a number of men of the first century, mostly drawn from the ordinary occupations of the time, fabricated the New Testament, with its penetrating insights into human nature, and with its amazing message of redemption from sin that is centred in the coming, the life and the death of Christ? To believe *that* is to demand more of credulity than our fourth doctrine demands of the Salvationist's faith.

Chapter Five

THE SIN OF MAN

5. *We believe that our first parents were created in a state of innocency, but by their disobedience they lost their purity and happiness; and that in consequence of their fall all men have become sinners, totally depraved; and as such are justly exposed to the wrath of God.*

IN the late 19th and early 20th centuries the use of the terms 'fall of man' and 'original sin' would have caused sceptical smiles in many high-brow circles. Those people nurtured a belief in the 'inevitable progress of mankind'. Today, however, living as we do in the wake of two world wars, there are evidences of greater realism. And indeed some of these 'intellectuals' have turned to the Christian faith primarily because it does declare these very truths.

If man is not 'fallen' how is it that he is 'down'? Can anyone today *doubt* that he is 'down'? Recall what this century has produced: the most brutal savagery in concentration and slave-labour camps; racial hatreds; a divorce rate that leads some sociologists to despair of marriage as an enduring institution; and the horrors of napalm, cluster bombs and so on—not to mention atom and hydrogen bombs.

Man's own record of progress is mainly along one line, that of scientific research – certainly not along moral and spiritual lines – and the stages of such progress are marked by the advent of new and more destructive weapons. Undoubtedly, man is 'down' and many fear that before long he will be 'out' as well, for now he has power completely to destroy himself. *Salvationists believe that his only hope lies in the clear recognition of his standing as a sinner before a holy, loving, personal God. Hence the relevance and validity of our fifth doctrine.*

Man always has been his own biggest problem and greatest enemy. Answers to the question, 'What is man?' are legion, with various assessments as diverse as can be imagined, from Swinburne's 'Glory to man in the highest for man is the master of things', to Nietzsche's 'Man is something that must be overcome'. Pascal was surely right when he wrote: 'Man knows not in what rank to place himself. He has evidently gone astray and fallen from his true place, unable to find it again.'

We live in a blighted world, and although there are problems in nature it is clear that the major part of the blight originates in man himself. The evil in a man's life needs explanation. It is much more important that he should understand the reason for his moral and spiritual failure than that he should know all about his physical origins.

We come then to the familiar problem of how to account for evil in a world made by a good God. The brief answer must be that the creation of freewill agents necessarily involved the *possibility* of evil – there had to be a real alternative. The state of our 'first parents' is described as 'innocency'. Their purity was no achievement of their own – it was something 'given'. And a moral agent needs a moral test. When the test came, our 'first parents' failed.

It is no good blaming our own failure on them. It is a strange paradox that while man cannot help being a sinner, his own conscience insists on his own guilt and responsibility. In the first century AD, when faithless men excused their moral derelictions on the ground of Adam's sin, a Jewish apocalyptist retorted: 'Each of us has been the Adam of his own soul.' This is in line with what a present-day theologian has written: 'The fall is a dimension of human experience which is always present. We are continually repudiating fellowship with God for which we were created. Every man is his own "Adam" and all men are solidarily "Adam".'

The doctrine of 'original sin' has been much misunderstood and often distorted. 'Total depravity' should not be made to carry the meaning of 'total corruption'. It means that the whole personality has been affected, and what applies to the individual applies equally to the whole human race. It should also be understood that 'original sin' does not mean 'original guilt', for guilt obviously cannot be transmitted.

It would be a mistake to imagine that it is possible to explain adequately the existence of moral evil in the world. We can only explain *the conditions under which it has become a stark reality*. In the story of Eden we note that the serpent, the mouthpiece of evil, was *already there*. And the same problem confronts us however far back we go in thought.

To explain evil adequately would be to make it rational, a reasonable thing – God-created. We would then have to fit it into a rational scheme of things and make it eternal. Determine fully the causes of a moral fact and it automatically ceases to be 'moral' and becomes a 'natural' fact, like gravitation or the beating of the heart. Moral evil remains as a completely irrational fact, and insoluble in an otherwise rational universe. Man's greatest need is a way of deliverance from sin and its consequences.

Chapter Six

THE ATONEMENT

6. *We believe that the Lord Jesus Christ has, by his suffering and death, made an atonement for the whole world, so that whosoever will may be saved.*

THIS statement, which is the heart of the Christian message, prompts a number of questions, but the two most important are: how did the death of Jesus make atonement, and how am I saved as a result of his death?

In facing the first of these questions we must be careful not to divorce the Cross from the revelation of God which Jesus brought. Too often the Cross has been fitted into a 'Judge-prisoner' rather than a 'Father-child' relationship, which was the essence of Jesus' teaching about God. Our relation to God is not a legal one, but a personal one.

Jesus and God are one. There can be no conflict in the Godhead. The death of Jesus did not *alter* God's attitude to us, it simply *revealed* it. The early Christians saw in his death the love of God. It was the grace of God that erected the Cross of Christ.

But why was the Cross necessary? One answer to this question, though by no means the only one, is that Jesus had to die so that sinful man might know the final truth about God. Truth is conveyed by words and deeds, and words are such inadequate things with which to describe God. Even *had* they been adequate, they need not be believed. They can but tell the truth; they cannot *convey* it, for they lack compelling power. If words had been equal to the task of conveying to man the truth about God, a book could have saved mankind. But no, the Word had to become flesh. And even Jesus' words were open to misunderstanding and misinterpretation. So the truth about God had to be unmistakably demonstrated. His love had to be put beyond all shadow of doubt.

Now Jesus *knew* the final truth about God. He knew that as soon as sin entered the world sorrow entered God's heart. 'He saw an infinite holiness bearing all sin's consequences, and fighting it with love and love alone.' In other words, he saw a Cross. His problem was this: how was mankind to see that Cross unless he brought it out of the invisible heart of God into the midst of this sinning world? 'The Cross was the most stupendous of all Christ's parables – a parable in flesh and blood.' It speaks the unutterable truth about God.

In a previous chapter we noted how evil arises out of man's misuse of his God-given freedom. From all eternity God was prepared to accept all the dire consequences of man's rebellion. The redemptive purpose of God has always been prepared for all the sacrifice its triumph might require. So, when man sinned, the historic Cross became a necessity, because *it was already present in the heart of God.* Jesus brought that Cross out of the Father-heart of God so that all mankind might be confronted with ultimate truth.

In the third chapter of John's Gospel we read:

God did not send his Son into the world to condemn the world, but to save the world through him ... This is the verdict: Light has come into the world, but men loved darkness instead of light because their deeds were evil (John 3:17, 19).

The *purpose* of Jesus' coming was salvation, but it inevitably brought judgment. The Cross judges us by revealing the awful truth about us, for it reveals the depths to which human depravity can go.

If man is to be saved he must begin by accepting the verdict that the Cross passes upon his sin, for they were ordinary, everyday sins that crucified Christ. They were not just first-century, but also 20th-century sins. That earlier age was no worse than this. Those men were no worse than we are. The Pharisees and Sadducees were, on balance, quite decent people. There is nothing about even Pilate or Caiaphas that is very different from ourselves. But how they all look in the light of the Cross! That is how *we* look in God's sight, and we must accept that judgment as the prelude to our salvation. We have nothing to contribute to our redemption save the sin from which we need to be redeemed.

How then does the Cross save man from his sin? The deadly thing about our past sins is not that they are past, but that they have become part of ourselves. Our sins have become our sinfulness. The only way to be saved is to be changed from what we are. It follows that we cannot be saved by anything that is merely external to ourselves, nor anything that is merely in the past. Salvationists believe that the life of Jesus, poured out in the sacrifice of death and released by the resurrection, is available to all who accept the condemnation that the Cross brings and see in it the visible pledge of what God is, and what he does for ever. By faith we can 'prove his death each day more healing'.

A final word: it is not our *view* of the atonement that saves, for there have been many varied theories. It is the *fact* of the atonement that saves, and the history and existence of the Christian Church, in spite of its many failings and weaknesses, bear adequate testimony to its abiding efficacy.

Chapter Seven
THE CONDITIONS OF SALVATION

7. *We believe that repentance toward God, faith in our Lord Jesus Christ and regeneration by the Holy Spirit are necessary to salvation.*

SALVATIONISTS are certain that man needs to be 'saved'.
For many today this is not a welcome truth, because it is a blow at their basic egotism. They would not object so strongly if they could persuade themselves that man could save himself, but *there is no evidence that points in this direction*. A religion of man's own make is worse than useless.

Meredith cried: 'More brains, O Lord, more brains!' While we would do well to echo that cry under certain circumstances, it must never be permitted to carry the meaning that man by his own applied intelligence can ever extricate himself from his spiritual predicament. Public Enemy Number One is not ignorance, or stupidity, or defective social environment, but *sin*. The trouble is *within* and only an inner transformation can deal with it.

Let us not be misled into imagining that current psychological techniques can cure man's spiritual ills. Because conversion is a psychological experience, and can therefore be psychologically *described* – in part, at least – it is not to be assumed that it can be either psychologically explained or induced. Applied psychology can improve mental health but it leaves the essential spiritual condition untouched.

Man is egocentric. All his thinking has a self-reference. He cannot, therefore, by more thought lose that self-reference. He cannot save himself. In the words of Samuel Daniel:

> *Unless above himself he can*
> *Erect himself, how poor a thing is man.*

Not only poor, but unsafe. Hence his need of salvation or, to return to the word of our seventh doctrine, regeneration.

There is a temptation to relegate the use of such words to people of disreputable character, but this must be resisted. The respectable *cannot* enter into a truly religious experience in any simpler, easier, uncritical way. We only need to recall that it was the wealthy, educated, cultured and *religious* Nicodemus, one of the recognised leaders of the Jewish nation, to whom Jesus said 'You must be born again' (John 3:7). A study of the context of that forthright declaration reveals that Jesus regarded Nicodemus as spiritually blind, impotent and sinful. We must beware of the ease with which respectability can be mistaken for essential virtue.

Christian doctrines must of necessity consist of generalisations; they cannot particularise. Christians must therefore be very careful not to allow any narrowness on their part to contradict the great variety of ways in which God woos and wins the hearts of men. 'The wind,' said Jesus, using it as a symbol of the Holy Spirit, who is always the agent in the work of grace, 'blows wherever it pleases. You hear its sound, but you cannot tell where it comes from, or where it is going' (John 3:8).

We believe, then, that God deals with every individual soul in a particular way, but having said this it is necessary to recognise the fact that, generally speaking, all men have the same primary need; hence it is both legitimate and necessary to generalise. So we declare that the 'conditions' of salvation are twofold – 'repentance toward God' and 'faith in our Lord Jesus Christ'. They form the prelude to 'regeneration by the Holy Spirit'.

A word must be said about each.

First of all, these 'conditions' are not arbitrarily imposed by God. He is not seeking to make men 'toe the line' before he will help them. *They are laws of the spiritual world.* No one can be saved except through repentance and faith, not because God refuses to act, but because it is by these means salvation comes. They delineate a condition of soul, and any other condition of soul keeps the gift of God's salvation at a distance. The gift is always there, just as there was forgiveness for Jesus' murderers *if they desired to avail themselves of it*. Repentance and faith are the means whereby the ever-offered gift is appropriated by the needy soul.

What then is meant by 'repentance'? It is certainly not just a matter of eating humble-pie. It means accepting God's standpoint in regard to sin, and that standpoint is seen in the Cross. It means bowing to that judgment. It means experiencing a sense of shame that is the beginning of the remaking of life. Repentance 'means unlearning all the self-conceit and self-will of years'. It is a description of what going back to God is like. But let us get this clear: this experience does not demoralise; it is the springboard of moral and spiritual action.

There are two kinds of faith: 'intellectual' faith and 'saving' faith. The former is included in the latter, for faith is not (as the schoolboy is reputed to have said) 'believing what you know to be untrue'! Psychologists differentiate between 'knowledge by description' and 'knowledge by acquaintance' and saving faith goes further than 'description'; it includes 'acquaintance'. It is personal commitment to Christ as Saviour and Lord.

Chapter Eight
JUSTIFICATION BY FAITH

8. *We believe that we are justified by grace through faith in our Lord Jesus Christ; and that he that believeth hath the witness in himself.*

'JUSTIFICATION by faith' is a magnificent phrase. It means so much to Protestantism, although it must be admitted that serious misunderstandings have sometimes gathered around it.

It does not mean that the believer is 'made' righteous, for righteousness is a quality of life that cannot be so imposed. What it does mean is that the believer is 'accounted' righteous, through no merits of his own for all is 'by grace' – and the way is thereby opened to a new life.

To illustrate from the best known of Jesus' parables: the prodigal son was 'justified' by his 'faith' in his father. As soon as he showed in action his belief in his father's love, he was treated as though the past had been obliterated, although we may well believe that some of the consequences of that past were still present and very real. The forgiveness of God deals with our personal relationship to himself, and does not automatically annul the cumulative results of our own wrongdoing.

In the same way as this beautiful parable illustrates, a man who takes Christ at his word is dealt with by God on a new basis, not because of what he has been (for that needs to be dealt with) or because of what he is (for this is the trouble) but because of what he is *on the road to become*. Justification is not an end, or a process, but a *beginning*.

'Justification' is a legal term, and it should be remembered that *all* terms, legal ones included, are inadequate when dealing with spiritual truth. One must never forget the intimate, personal nature of man's relationship with God.

W. N. Clarke wrote:

Grace sets right our legal relation to God but only by making it cease to be legal ... the essence of God's pardon is in showing himself so gracious as to give us faith in his love, and it is in this sense that we are justified by faith.

Faith is a discernment by men of the mind and heart of God, and by it we enter into an experience of his grace.

Writing about Jesus' attitude to publicans and sinners, H. R. Mackintosh said:

Being what he was he gave them the pardoning friendship of God by bringing God to them in a power and reality that awed and cleansed the soul. Salvation met them not as a new requirement, more exacting by far than the old; it was a gift, rather, capable of making them new persons in a new world.

The primary thing in Jesus' presentation of himself as Saviour lay in his forgiving attitude toward sinners, and in his ability to convey to needy souls the assurance that his own loving mind toward them was in deed and truth the mind of God.

Salvation does not come to men by virtue of their moral excellence, their noble character or their good works (although salvation should *produce* these things), but by a trustful acceptance of the fact that 'God was reconciling the world to himself in Christ, not counting men's sins against them' (2 Corinthians 5:19), ie by 'accounting' them as righteous. Men and women can do nothing to merit salvation – it is the gift of God's grace.

The Christian view is that the only really good man or woman is the one who has been pardoned, and that person is good because he or she has been delivered from that self-centredness which underlies all moral and spiritual failure. Such a person is content to owe everything to God, even the grace that led him or her to an appreciation of their need, and the faith whereby the forgiveness of God was mediated to their heart. We have nothing that we have not received.

Spurgeon used to tell the story of a minister who called on a poor woman with money to help pay her rent. She kept the door locked, pretending to be out, because she thought it was the landlord calling *for* the rent. The summons she refused to obey was not 'rent demanded', but 'rent paid'. So it is when God challenges us – the only demand he makes is that we shall be willing to receive.

Perhaps this was the real point of Jesus' use of a child as an illustration of man's need of conversion. It was not the child's innocence and simplicity that he was trying to teach. It was the child's sense of utter dependence, the willingness frankly and openly to receive gifts, the absence of false pride. 'Do not be afraid, little flock,' said Jesus; 'for your Father has been pleased to *giv*e you the Kingdom' (Luke 12:32).

Chapter Nine

THE WAY OF OBEDIENCE

9. *We believe that continuance in a state of salvation depends upon continued obedient faith in Christ.*

THIS statement constitutes a warning. It is a reminder that after the experience of regeneration, freewill is still a reality. Christian in John Bunyan's *Pilgrim's Progress* saw that there was a path to perdition from the very gates of the Celestial City. No experience of divine grace absolves us from the obligation to keep ourselves always within the will and purpose of God. Jesus could say of his followers, 'No-one can snatch them out of my Father's hand' (John 10:28), yet it is always possible for the follower to *take himself* out of the divine will. The true believer is invulnerable to *external* attack, but at any moment part of his own nature may turn traitor to the whole, may capitulate to the enemy of his soul; and the result will be spiritual collapse.

Temptation is a stark reality in the Christian life. It invariably begins in the realm of the mind, and it is there the battle must be fought and won. While all in our spiritual experience is of God's grace, there is here a place for effort and discipline.

With glad abandon the song of experience can be sung:

> *'Tis done, the great transaction's done!*
> *I am my Lord's and he is mine.*

But that past 'transaction' must be ratified in the everyday, and of this the final verse reminds us:

High Heaven, that heard the solemn vow,
That vow renewed shall daily hear.

There are those who hold the opposite point of view – that once a person has experienced salvation he is eternally secure. To us this seems to imply that God's great gift of freedom is annulled, which carries with it the corollary that the goodness which flows from the experience is automatic and inevitable. This is plainly an unacceptable notion, for 'automatic goodness' is a contradiction in terms. In order to be truly good a man must be free, aware, responsive to suggestions, able to hear the various voices calling him to this and that. The happiness of a good man rests largely upon the realisation that he might have been otherwise.

Salvationists believe that at any moment a man may go back upon that initial act of repentance and faith which constitutes the 'wicket gate' leading to the new way of life. He can in an instant of weakness or folly make a decision that will destroy the spiritual edifice he has been erecting.

Someone, in answer to what has been written above, may be tempted to quote the New Testament to the effect that believers are called upon to live the eternal life *here and now* (John 5:24; 17:2, 3). This is true. The citizen of the Kingdom of Heaven must remember his citizenship, just as a traveller living far from the traditions and disciplines of home should not deny his homeland. But this does not alter the fact that he *can* give way to temptation. Likewise the citizen of Heaven can deny his citizenship, and by denying lose it.

Others may say that believers are called to *receive* the *end* of their faith, even the salvation of their souls (1 Peter 1:9, *KJV*), and this also is true. This New Testament statement, however, must not be made to carry a denial of the idea of progression in the religious life, or to contradict the doctrine we are here considering. It simply means that the whole future of the spiritual life is given in its beginning. It is *implicit* as a principle, but it must become *explicit* in the unfolding life, hence the need for 'continued obedient faith in Christ'.

Obedience is the organ of vision. Those who *do* God's will *know* the doctrine, for they have an experimental, if not a theoretical, understanding of it. Christ's call is to a life of following and his promise is being verified constantly: 'Whoever follows me, will never walk in darkness, but will have the light of life' (John 8:12).

Man is often beset with a desire for a particular kind of certainty that is a grave spiritual danger. He may even renounce his freedom in order to escape from responsibility and thus feel 'safe'. Christianity does not capitulate to this human desire. It calls men to a responsible life of tension and hazard, but withal it can be a life of constant inner victory.

Here is a call to adventurous living. There is no sense of having finally 'arrived', for this would lead to stagnation. The future is wide open with glorious possibilities, but the warning note of this ninth doctrine must be ever borne in mind.

Leave no unguarded place,
No weakness of the soul;
Take every virtue, every grace,
And fortify the whole.
(Charles Wesley, SASB 695)

Chapter Ten

THE SANCTIFIED LIFE

10. *We believe that it is the privilege of all believers to be 'wholly sanctified' and that their 'whole spirit and soul and body' may 'be preserved blameless unto the coming of our Lord Jesus Christ' (I Thessalonians 5:23, KJV).*

A VARIETY of terms is used to describe the experience of sanctification. We speak of 'the blessing of holiness', 'the blessing of a clean heart', 'the experience of perfect love' and 'the second blessing'.

Salvationists do not believe that God intends the believer to be for ever frustrated, dissatisfied, unequal to life. On the contrary, we believe that God intends his people to be equal to every challenge, and for this purpose his grace has been made available to all. Where sin abounded grace can 'much more abound' (see Romans 5:20, *KJV*).

This doctrine has its genesis in the character of God. Because God is holy, holiness is his requirement of man. His holiness makes ours imperative. 'Be holy, because I am holy' (1 Peter 1:16).

It is of the utmost importance that it should be realised that *because* God is holy, man can be the same. Man's holiness is dependent upon God's. It is the gift of his grace, and not man's own achievement. Man is privileged to share what God is. The only righteousness man can achieve is *self*-righteousness, which is the most effective of barriers separating man from God. Man's only hope of holiness lies in an attitude of humble receptivity.

'Holiness' and 'sanctification' might seem forbidding words, but it is of value constantly to remind oneself that what we mean by them has been fully expressed in the character of Jesus Christ. He is the plumbline let down from Heaven. He is man's incorruptible conscience. In him we see the eternal beauty of God, and the supreme wonder is that through him this beauty can be imparted as the crown of life to man. Because of his victory in the realm of the flesh, the realm that evil has claimed as its own domain, he has brought into that realm the unimpaired power of the Spirit of God. Jesus is God, in all God's power and holiness, made available for man, in all his weakness and sin.

God's demand of holiness is made reasonable because of his willingness to *bestow* it on those whose consecration is entire. It is only those who hunger and thirst after righteousness who are satisfied. By God's grace the sinner is accepted, but the purpose of that grace is not to set aside God's demand of holiness. It is rather to *further* that demand by bringing it within the realm of possibility.

It should not be imagined that belief in the possibility of a holy life involves 'perfectionism'. When the experience of sanctification comes to man he is but at the beginning of a developing spiritual life. The experience does not kill idealism, but enlivens it; it does not mean an end of aspiration, but a quickening of it. The religious life is a process: it is life tending God-ward; it can never have an absolute end this side of the grave. At all costs Paul's 'forward-looking' outlook must be preserved. Nearing the end of his life he wrote to the Philippians:

Not that I have already obtained all this, or have already been made perfect, but I press on to take hold of that for which Christ Jesus took hold of me. Brothers, I do not consider myself yet to have taken hold of it. But one thing I do: Forgetting what is behind and straining toward what is ahead, I press on toward the goal to win the prize for which God has called me heavenward in Christ Jesus (Philippians 3:12–14).

Seeing holiness is Christlikeness, there will always be plenty of room for improvement, for advancement, for endless development in our personal lives. Yet, if a man lives in harmony with God's revealed will, having no sense of condemnation, at *each point* of his spiritual development there will be a certain 'completeness'. God is at the beginning of our spiritual pilgrimage, he is with us each point of the way, yet there is a sense in which we are journeying *toward* him. Here we have a paradox which bears the hallmark of truth.

This, too, can be said: there is a perfection of *intention* although the achievement may fall woefully short. We may say of the child who, in a desire to help, does more harm than good, that we accept 'the will for the deed'. So God in his mercy applauds the sincere intention even though the performance itself may be pitiable. We are called to live 'blamelessly', and this is possible. Were we called to live 'faultlessly', we might well despair.

When the vital experience of sanctification takes place, the old life, the raw material of natural desire, is only present as a foreign, alien thing. The inmost spirit identifies itself with the *true* self, the new life. Evil, error, imperfection, no longer belong to us, but are outgrowths with no organic relation to our true nature. They are aspects of life which are already virtually, and eventually will actually be, suppressed and annulled.

Paul urges: 'In the same way, count yourselves dead to sin, but alive to God in Christ Jesus' (Romans 6:11). The sanctified man does not sin wilfully, but regards himself as dead to all that. Continually he refuses to recognise as in any sense his own those factors that would deny Christ in his life. The accent of his life is no longer on the 'I', but on Christ who saves a man from himself.

Chapter Eleven

LAST THINGS

11. *We believe in the immortality of the soul; in the resurrection of the body; in the general judgment at the end of the world; in the eternal happiness of the righteous and in the endless punishment of the wicked.*

THE final doctrine of The Salvation Army deals, appropriately, with 'last things'. Here we are immediately confronted with the lamentable inadequacy of words, for human speech is linked with the world of time and space and cannot cope fully with ultimate matters. Whatever we may mean by such a term as the 'end of history', it will be an act of God, a supra-historical event, and as such must be by its very nature largely inconceivable to us. We tend to think of eternity in terms of 'future time' but this is really symbolic language, for eternity is really a condition *outside* time.

In view of the difficulties, the temptation to cease bothering about such matters might prove irresistible, and yet it is only by seeking to relate passing events to an 'absolute end' that real meaning and significance can be given to the whole process.

Death is more certain than life. It is in fact the one event in our personal future of which we can be quite sure, and making sense of life means making sense of death.

Salvationists, then, believe in the immortality of the soul. For one thing, without such a concept life in time is without meaning, goal, purpose or significance. It is nothing.

We see life as a 'principle of individuation'. Throughout the whole creative process God has been aiming at the creation of individual human personalities; and we cannot believe that when the particles of matter forming the human body disintegrate, the soul, the real person, ceases to exist. Matter is incapable of producing mind and spirit, but can only provide the vehicle of its expression in this kind of world.

Belief in immortality is sometimes attributed to man's egotism – he cannot think of himself as passing out of existence! Our Christian faith has its basis elsewhere, in the revelation of God in Christ. With compelling force he revealed that God loves every soul of man, and it is in that love that man's immortality rests. To believe otherwise would be to malign the character of God.

It is said sometimes that the ideal of immortality was chiefly Greek in origin, but the idea of the resurrection of the body was Jewish. Many today will regard the former as a possibility, but look askance on the latter. This is due mainly to a misunderstanding of what is meant by the phrase.

Paul said quite definitely that 'flesh and blood cannot inherit the kingdom of God' (1 Corinthians 15:50), and introduced the term 'spiritual body' (v. 44). Here again the limitations of language are experienced. Paul used the illustration of the sown seed, and declared 'God gives it a body as he has determined' (1 Corinthians 15:38), thus emphasising the *difference* between what is sown and what grows from it.

This doctrine is a picture taken from our present experience to express a conception of the completion of life transcending our experience. Eternity will not be the cancellation of time and history, but its fulfilment. The deeds done in the body carry an eternal significance, and Christ will bring whole men into a complete relationship with God.

When rightly understood the fact of judgment gives dignity to human life. Man being immortal must come under the judgment of eternity – he cannot just ooze out of life!

Christ is both the Person who will judge us, and the standard of judgment. By taking flesh and entering history he has won the right to do so. Indeed we can say that men simply judge themselves by not being like him. Because of the Incarnation 'the history of the world is the judgment of the world' – and this is true both corporately and individually.

In thinking about Heaven we are back at our initial problem, for we have only earthly language to describe unearthly things. Our attempts at description may even distort the truth we are trying to make plain.

Rupert Brooke wrote a humorous poem on the fishes' idea of Heaven. If it were possible for a fish to imagine a fishy heaven it would, of course, think in terms of 'wetter water' and 'slimier slime', and a place where 'there shall be no more land'! The point to realise is that while our minds are to be trusted within their limits, they do have their limits, and in thinking about Heaven we are trying to escape the limits of the three-dimensional world in which we are placed.

It may be best to try to think of Heaven as a state or condition, rather than as a place. The New Testament teaches that we *have* eternal life. It is here hampered by the world, the flesh and the devil, but *then* we will enjoy it without any hindrance whatsoever. 'And so we will be with the Lord for ever' (1 Thessalonians 4:17) – that is enough for faith, and wisdom will leave the matter there.

Many reject the doctrine of Hell out of hand. It is a frivolous modern heresy that everything is bound to come right in the end. This attitude demonstrates a lack of thoroughness in a person's thinking. If free-will is a reality, Hell must be a possibility.

But let this be said: Hell is never the will of God, for 'He is patient with you, not *wanting* anyone to perish' (2 Peter 3:9). The sufferings of those who persist in rejecting God's love in Christ are *self-imposed*, for they have contracted out of Heaven. Evil judges itself. The penalty is the recoil of the sin. 'All the punishments of God are self-acting; they are not inflicted, they follow.'

In concluding these brief studies let this be said: *Within* our faith there is plenty of room for new vision and revelation. On many points we have to say 'I do not know', but one thing we do know – Christ is for us the experimental answer to all of life's personal issues. Because of him we have no moral problem at the heart of our universe. With Paul, we may know only 'in part', but the 'part' we do know is Jesus Christ, and he is sufficient.